The Art of Hitting Home Runs

Tyler Cook

Tyler Cook

The Art of Hitting Home Runs

Tyler Cook

The Art of Hitting Home Runs

Copyright © 2018 Tyler Cook.
All rights reserved.

This book may not be reproduced, in whole or in part, in any form or by any means mechanical or electronic, including photocopying, recording, or by any information storage retrieval system now known or hereafter invented, without written permission from the author, Tyler Cook.

ISBN: 978-1-729-00177-6

Tyler Cook

The Art of Hitting Home Runs

Contents

Chapter 1
Chapter 2
Chapter 3
Chapter 4
Chapter 5
Chapter 6
Chapter 7
Chapter 8
Chapter 9

Tyler Cook

1

A hitter who loves hitting home runs will hit more throughout a lifetime. One can hit a home run every game. Know it. When the ecstasy of hitting a home run is paired with the player's passion, it will happen quite frequently. I know this gratifying experience firsthand. The enlightening information mentioned herein is intended to maximize home runs. This manifesto is what I've discovered to work best for me.

When I was a 12-year old little leaguer, I hit 29 homers in 25 games. To put this in perspective, Mark McGwire hit 13 home runs in a little league season. I've never met another person who has hit more than 29. It's rare to find a modern little leaguer in the Little League World Series with homerun totals remotely comparable to mine. I've read about a couple players who hit in the 30s after playing through the entire LLWS. So they had many more at-bats. I am probably in the top 3 of all-time for most little league home runs.

At age 13, I attended the Roberto Clemente All-Stars baseball camp in Florida. Major League Baseball MVP: Andrew McCutchen was a 13-year-old camp attendee too. I won the home run derby for my age group. I hit a home run in my first at-bat in the first of several exhibition games. I remember the scouts paying special attention to McCutchen even at such a young age and deservingly so.

I was the most offensive hitter my high school had ever statistically witnessed. I went on to break the majority of my high school baseball team's hitting records. In my freshman and sophomore varsity years combined, I produced similar statistics to fellow Ohio sensation Ken Griffey Jr. And, at age 17 was recruited by The University of Miami in Florida. It was arguably the best university for baseball in the United States at the time. Alex Rodriguez almost attended it, but wisely chose to go straight to the majors instead.

The Art of Hitting Home Runs

By my mid-teens, I'd lost the passion for baseball along with the love for hitting home runs and chose not to play baseball at a collegiate level. Passion is a fusion of love and hate. It is invaluable in baseball players. Nevertheless I still retain the knowledge of what makes a great home run hitter. As I've matured as a person, I've learned additional lifestyle adjustments I wished I had implemented when I was an everyday player.

I am grateful to share my lifestyle views to help others benefit. It is my intention to speak on what factors into habitual home run success in an effort to improve your game and in raising your consciousness.

People may say hitting home runs is about natural talent, great physical size and strength. These things all help, but are not prerequisites. Cleveland Indians slugger, José Ramírez stands at a height of 5'9", but is a league leader in home runs. Former MVP: Dustin Pedroia is listed at the same height (probably shorter) and was a leader in slugging percentage. All-time great home run hitters, Willie Mays, Mel Ott and Yogi Berra stood a similar short stature. Anyone can hit home runs regularly regardless of physical prowess.

Tyler Cook

The capacity to hit walloping dingers is a stunning ability many hitters endeavor to enhance. The approaches to maximize going yard may not be as obvious as you initially may think. I have seen many solid hitters who are great on a bench press or moving weight around the weight room, yet cannot find a way to touch 'em all with one swing. On the flipside, I have seen players that don't know where the weight room is, but can hit blasts practically to the next zip code.

Most scouts and mangers have to use quantifiable means in finding a great home run hitter or a decent player in general. They look at size, tract bat speed, strength and analyze all sorts of numbers to justify who is worth pursuing. Those attributes are advantageous, but aren't the greatest assets for hitting homers. The most valuable quality of a home run hitter is intangible. It is "the edge." Few players actually possess it. It is in the realm of excessive confidence yet beneath arrogance.

There is a humbly confident self-awareness mixed with respect and assertiveness in those who have the edge. It is not easily identifiable, even by a peer, because it is intrapersonal. Confidence is ubiquitous among star hitters. But when a hitter has the edge, he is indomitable.

The Art of Hitting Home Runs

The bulk of the content contained in this book is eye-opening alternative information for how to hit home runs. It is provocative knowledge. Listening to mainstream advice will produce mediocre results in most facets of life. Hitting home runs is no different. In order to be a prolific home run hitter, don't have a normal routine and approach to becoming one. Choose an abnormal one.

The power of visualization can yield wonderful results. Before hitting my enrapturing first in game over-the-fence home run, I did toss-ups to myself. I actually hit a self-tossed home run as a right-handed hitter. It sparked an awakening in me. The most important part about this situation was actually seeing the ball go over the fence off of my bat. I no longer had to imagine I could hit a home run, I knew it with absolute conviction.

I replayed this in my mind with that satisfying, euphonious crack of the bat a home run hitter is all too familiar with for the rest of the day. Doing so further reinforced the likelihood of similar visions in my future.

The following day I had a baseball game. I veraciously spoke about this recent breakthrough home run to my teammates. One of them didn't believe me at all. It angered me. I didn't realize it, but I used this anger and transmuted it into the euphoria of hitting the home run. I felt angry about what the teammate said and visualized hitting the home run as I did the night before. The evocative experience served me well. Afterward I let it all go and moved on to play the game.

I didn't think about either situation during the live game and focused on playing. Sure enough I hit a home run mid way through the game. It was surreal.

More home runs give more mental references and create habitual threads in the mind. The brain strives for normalcy. If hitting home runs every game is the new normal, the brain will more than likely figure out how to keep it that way.

Journaling is quite empowering. I am a strong advocate of it because it has a correlation with peak performance. Once I felt confident in my power hitting ability I began journaling about it. Soon I had a revelation: I could hit a home run every game. I continued composing handwritten entries after my new paradigm shift.

Throughout the entire baseball season as a 12 year old I documented every game with a short summary of each at-bat. I included anything noteworthy about the game in brief sentences. Including emotions when journaling is helpful. I didn't include many emotions in those journal entries though. I hadn't acquired much toxic buildup or emotional debris at that time. Younger people usually are more in touch with their bodies and clearer inside.

    A body scan is great if you don't know what you're feeling. When an area of the body has pain or tension, question what emotion it might be linked with and write it in the journal entry. This simple act avoids stagnant energy buildup and keeps the body's energetic circulatory flow at a healthy current.

Hitting a baseball well is an agile, flowing athletic movement. An ideal swing activates a series of kinetic movements. Hitters must know when to keep still too. We see many exalted hall-of-fame caliber hitters keeping their heads still while batting. Their shoulders don't move until necessary either.

    A "hitch" (dropping of the hands) was helpful for developing my timing and rhythm. Each hitter personalizes their distinct hitch. I naturally evolved my own. I held my hands above my shoulder, below my ear and dropped them just beneath my pectoral muscle while waiting for the incoming pitch delivery.

Power hitting is a reflection of synergy. Allowing the energetic and physical bodies to work in unison with supreme verve will put an adequate amount of energy into the baseball, resulting in a home run. Drawing up this energy is vital. Letting it flow through the body bestows animation to the swing and transfers the energy upon impact.

Before the wind up and pitch, it is imperative to concentrate energy in the back calf muscle and the ball of the back foot; left foot for the left handed batter. It's a way of powering-up. This charges and builds the energy up with excessive intensity, essentially lighting a fire in the muscle. It gets exhausted quickly. So, only do it for several seconds before the pitch.

It is the sacrosanct impetus for hitting home runs. It enables a massive weight shift to occur during the swing followed by explosive contact with the ball, leading to longer distance hits and deep fly home run bombs.

2

As long as the pitcher throws strikes, a home run can be hit. I know this with every fiber of my being and trust it. Eventually a home run pitch is coming. This emboldens the player to be patient, especially once the ability to hit the baseball square is mastered. The home run hitter protects the strike zone. It is his domain. Anything he doesn't want in it must be sent away. Once the intuition is fine-tuned and honed in, it knows a potential home run pitch immediately.

Being humble is to be humane and relate to the lower forms of thyself, humans and earth's life forms. There is great power in humility. The aforementioned base of the hitter's power is in his footing, so he must stay humble and grounded to continue stellar play. He is in touch with both his lower and higher nature. If the hitter gets too high or prideful, he no longer has the foundation of his lower humble self and can topple over in arrogance.

Great home run hitters are both patient and aggressive respectively, playing with decisive action free of hesitation when selecting the pitch. Do not think when looking for a home run pitch. It throws the intuition off-line. The intuition is an incredible selector. It triggers the swing. Trust it. Great hitters, like great leaders are assertive and decisive. They decide quickly and change their minds slowly.

Many hitters are pitch 'guessers". I am not. Guessing may work better for right-handed hitters because their questioning/logical side of their brain is more dominant. Thinking and guessing is synonymous with doubt. I never recommend this unless attempting to make contact. Home run hitters look for their pitch to hit out-of-the park.

Being tentative about making contact or striking out is not a thought in the home run hitter's mind. Hitter's may get concerned with what the manager, base coach, or other players might think about situational hitting. Those people do have authority. But when you're in the batter's box you make all the executive decisions and no one else. Play with backbone and it will serve you well. Hitting home runs is about stepping into your own authority.

I am a lefty. Left-handed hitters have a better chance at hitting home runs often. The ballparks are usually favored for a left-hander to pull a home run. The wall is generally closer. The main reason lefties can hit home runs more easily is using the right brain hemisphere. This side of the brain is linked to the left side of the body. It deals with knowing, intuition and flow. It is more natural and geared toward ascetics too, making left-handers look more comfortable, natural and fluid at bat.

Batting left-handed puts the hitter more in touch with his feelings as opposed to a righty. This is important in sorting out the pitches better. It makes the hitter empathic to each pitch. It makes feeling confident easier. Constructing visualizations in the brain are more easily accessed while batting too.

In Neuro-Linguistic Programming, we know the brain accesses different regions based on where the eyes are focused. When the eyes look to the upper right corner (where the pitcher is for a lefty batter) it accesses the part of the brain associated with visual construction.

It depends on the person's brain wiring, but scientists discovered in NLP most people access their kinesthetic portion of the brain by looking to their right too. This brain region allows the person to perceive their bodily movements and sensations better. It's an ideal region to access while hitting a baseball.

This is a more confortable eye movement for reading English as well. Readers can feel the emotional context of the story better because the sentences are read left to right. Cinematographers use this same tactic in movies and videos. They have the good guy come on screen from left to right and the bad guy enter vice versa.

Righties are more mechanical. Their dominant brain hemisphere is concerned with thinking, guessing, and analyzing. Right-handed hitters can obviously still hit home runs. However, it's not as easy to access the flow state. Lefties are more conducive to the flow state.

The flow state is a powerful state of mind in the brain's right-hemisphere, where the lefty naturally dwells. It's extemporaneous. Like, speaking from the heart. Being in the flow state makes the hitter an open conduit. It allows the energy charge in the calf muscle/ball of the foot to circulate throughout the body rapidly. Then instantly release this luminosity as a massive force on the ball. Upon the discharge, the force is exerted, but it emanates from a source of power. The hitter is not actually forcing anything to happen.

The Art of Hitting Home Runs

Hitting home runs is a masculine act. The masculine-feminine polarity in the individual is beneficial for the hitter. Increasing the masculine energy will enhance the feminine energy because the feminine is drawn to the masculine. The feminine energy heightens the intuition for selecting and receiving pitches well. When the masculine energy is tapped into, the feminine energy magnetically amplifies. The feminine will assist in the flow of the life force throughout the body radiating from the rear calf, while the masculine will facilitate the release of it.

The integration of masculinity and femininity is symbolized in the literal baseball, as the ball is stitched together resembling the yin-yang symbol. The duality of the game attempts to split the players identities between teams and left/right sides of the plates, but the home run hitter is not split inside. He is integrated.

Give special attention to the lower body in workouts. Many people initially think hitting is about upper body strength and the fitness of the lower body is overlooked. This is a bumbling error. When you are swinging your bat, your legs and core are assuming the role of supporting your swing and adding power to it. The lower body will enable you to magnify that additional piece of intensity and further augment the amount of round trippers.

 The bulk of the robust energy in the swing comes from the lower half of the body: the feet, legs, thighs and hips. The lower region generates torque for power hitting. Arm strength is secondary to planting your foot. The hands and forearms play an important role too though.

 The best kept secret for hitting more home runs is harnessing sexual energy. I was oblivious to this revelation of carnal knowledge until later in life. One could debate the act of hitting a home run is sexual.

 Sperm is potent life force energy. It can be used to create a human being or beget home runs. Without an ejaculation, even only several days of retention amps the testosterone levels up extremely high and forms a plateau after about a week.

 Higher testosterone heightens the masculine energy. Semen retention has a positive effect on the brain after a while. The unused life force energy ascends up the spine into the brain. It then enhances cognitive functioning to an optimal degree.

The Art of Hitting Home Runs

As a 12-year-old boy who'd reached puberty and retained my semen, I was able to use it for hitting home runs. And the home run totals were quite bountiful. In high school baseball, my overall athletic performance and home run totals dropped, subsequent to regular sexual engagements with girlfriends.

It is important to maintain a higher vibration to accrue more home runs, so any person who merges energies with a home run hitter must be of equal or higher resonance. If not, the vibratory rate of the home run hitter will lower, making hitting home runs less easy. Basically have sex with high quality people and people you wouldn't mind living their lives. If not, your home runs totals could plummet. The right partner will complement and be supportive energetically.

Another brilliant tactic to naturally skyrocket testosterone is by taking cold showers. Additional endorphins in the brain are released and coordination is briefly improved. Starting the shower at a warm temperature and gradually changing the water to lukewarm and eventually cold will suffice.

Cold showers are an affordable version of whole-body cryotherapy. LeBron James uses cryotherapy — the utilization of sub zero temperatures to treat tissues. The world's fastest man, Usain Bolt and soccer star Cristiano Ronaldo are a few world-class athletes known to take advantage of ultra low temperatures.

      A stimulating cold shower of only a minute or two is enough to expedite healing. Testosterone, endorphins, rapid muscle recovery, increased circulation, and long term fat burning are all perks of this simple daily act. Body builders are known to take cold showers before competitions. It's hyper refreshing and the stress easily rolls off of you throughout the day.

The Art of Hitting Home Runs

3

Baseball players go through ups and downs in their seasons. A superstitious mind can arise in the troughs. This won't bode well for the aspiring grand magus of grand slams. When a home run hitter goes through a drought of home runs or even of getting hits, he or she may develop superstitions. This is indicative of the home run hitter being thrown off of the masculine core. Now the power is being placed on external things such as, certain socks or a special bat etc. It means the hitter is letting the outside influences control him.

    I believe it is important to accessorize and wear certain articles of clothing when it increases confidence. However, I disagree with using these as a superstitious reason for success. A true home run king has massive internal value and force. All of his power is sourced from within his essence.

We often see professional baseball players wearing chains and an assortment of jewelry. People can dismiss it as flash, but it's much deeper. Jewelry designs can have a calming effect or quite the opposite.

When a pitcher sees a ring on a hitter's hand it has multiple connotations. The pitcher knows if he hits the batter with a pitch, the unfortunate event of a brawl could ensue. A punch from a hitter wearing a ring will be dangerous and potentially lethal, just as a wild pitch could be. The pitcher knows it subconsciously. It makes him tentative and more likely to throw strikes, usually unaware of the true reason.

Adding accessories to the uniform is self-expression. Any art form is about expressing and hitting home runs is an art. Expression is liberating and keeps the hitter's mind and body limber. Accessorizing with the appropriate jewelry is great for the home run hitter. These can be agents assisting in the player's individuation within the unit of the team.

Sunglasses are recommended apparel while hitting. These can help boost confidence, protect the eyes from harmful ultraviolet rays, and relax the eyes and extraocular muscles. When the eyes are comfortable it's easier to read the pitches.

The Art of Hitting Home Runs

The average player is not a home run hitter. Obviously all players have uniforms. Customize yours in a fashion suitable to you and your interpretation of who a home run hitter really is. Numerology definitely factors into the game of baseball more than it meets the eye. An appropriate number on the back of the jersey can amplify the individual's power hitting performance. There isn't a perfect number for everyone. Numbers emit an energetic frequency like anything else.

A home run king accesses his power internally and is usually drawn to regal jewelry such as gold to help stabilize his higher vibratory rate. Everything vibrates. All frequencies in the surrounding environment influence one another. Metals and gems not only have an intrinsic value, but a more solid frequency. It is more likely for a person to attune to that frequency because it is stable, where as a human being is in constant flux.

Gold attracts a divine healing frequency and will help the home run hitter operate at a higher frequency and avoid slumps. Home run kings are often drawn to gold chains and rings. Gold is linked with the sun and masculinity. Wearing gold jewelry is perfect for drawing in more masculine energy. It is great for blood circulation throughout the body. Copper sleeves do this to a lesser degree and are more affordable. These reduce muscle and joint pains. The gold and copper will free up the energy and stop inhibiting any energy flow.

A badass home run hitter rules the field, puts out an impression and at the helm, creates the environment of a champion. Clothing is part of our environment. Paying attention to the ingredients in athletic apparel is important, because any chemicals in the clothing or laundry detergent will be absorbed from the fabric into the pores. Don't wear deodorant either. It has toxic chemicals and suppresses. Positive emotions appeal to all senses. Confident hitters smell amazing.

If not mindful about these minute details, the hitter can be thrown off his core and out of balance inhibiting self-expression.

A grounding stone, such as tiger's eye or obsidian on a bracelet or necklace will help anchor you in the batter's box. A grounded hitter is more physically balanced and energetically integrated. An adequate physical balance makes the weight shift seamless during the swing, contact and follow-through. The specific stones for grounding and harmony may vary for each person. Finding the right stone or jewelry that speaks to the hitter is almost always the appropriate one.

The Art of Hitting Home Runs

Essential oils are great for sustaining a high vibration. The home run hitter can remedy physical and emotional issues with the regular use of the oils. I personally recommend frankincense. It is the essential oil of kings. It helps the home run king stay sharp mentally and doesn't let a tiny slump or a slew of striking out bother him for long. It gives the hitter more presence, serenity and emotional balance. It has a magnetizing effect too. People are drawn to the wearer of it.

The surrounding environment will respond to frankincense like the regal aroma it truly is by entraining up to it, or subliminally submitting to it and the wearer. Ideally the pitcher will be slightly more likely to submit. A few drops rubbed on the forearms or a drop or two under the tongue is exponentially beneficial. It's a subtlety, but a powerful one in the long term, nonetheless. Lavender is my second favorite essential oil.

Growing facial hair and lengthy hair on the head will help absorb more energy to facilitate home run production. Facial hair absorbs more masculine solar energy from the sun and vitamin D. The hitter will have higher testosterone and aggression.

There is a lunar center in the chin area. This is a port of reception for energetic influences. Facial hair on the chin will make the hitter more emotionally stable at the plate because the facial hair blocks the external influence of this energy. A great home run hitter wants output from oneself over input from external sources.

I had a thin mustache at age 12. I did because I didn't have a razor and wasn't shaving yet. It's funny to think about in retrospect, but it was helping me hit better. A mustache helps boost aggression and testosterone a tiny amount too. It could induce a slightly manic phase. It makes me prone to feel overconfident. Overall it is probably better to have a full beard to anchor the mustache and emotional state.

Hair length on the top of the head enhances intuition. This is well known in the military. Cutting off too much hair impairs the intuition and makes the person more submissive, impressionable and easily controlled. Native American seekers with long hair were recruited by the military to warn the armies of approaching danger. These people were sought specifically for their abilities to feel out the predators. Both the military and the seekers credit this to their hair length.

The Art of Hitting Home Runs

At least several inches grown off the top of the head is recommended. Anywhere for 4-12 inches will enhance athletic performance. When selecting a great home run pitch, the intuition must be active. I hit the most home runs with hair length near my eyebrows. Micro antennas are formed on the hairs. These pick up additional information and readily process it in the human brain.

A strong surge of confidence mixed with innate decisive action is attributed to the player's intuitive competence. It's as if an alert is triggered with a higher volume and intensity when the intuition is heightened. Knowing the home run pitch is blatantly obvious.

4

During every at-bat the hitter must remain present. Staying up in the head and overthinking is dense and cancerous to a prolific home run hitter. Hitters can think to assess the situation outside of the box, but never within it. Presence gives the energy fluidity and stops the ego from constricting the hitter. Knowing your intention to hit a home run before every game is enough. Once the energy is charged in the calf/ball of foot, the hitter can merely swing and allow the drawn up energy surge to work it's magic.

An awe-inspiring slugger doesn't try to hit home runs. He targets the pitch, swings and it happens. If the ego takes over the mind of the hitter, it can be beneficial in the short-term and catastrophic in the long-term. In the short-term the ego can give a boost of confidence or arrogance to muscle home runs. In the long run it feeds on validation. The home run hitter can become addicted to it.

The home run hitter must not trade away value for validation. The internal value of the home run hitter, which is his greatest source of power is syphoned off by the ego. It is far better to stay present and love hitting home runs instead of chasing the validation and the elation of actually homering. A true home run king sees the beauty in the entire process of hitting the home run and loves it passionately.

Be a lark. Waking up early can vastly increase your home run production and mood, especially with sun gazing. I played better when I feel asleep between 10 and 10:30 pm. Getting out of bed at sunrise will give an awaken person more exposure to sunlight throughout the day. The air is fresher and the brain absorbs more oxygen in the morning.

Quality of sleep, maintaining circadian rhythm and absorbing as much light as possible is better than the quantity of sleeping hours. Each hour of sleep before midnight is equivalent to 2 hours of sleep after midnight. It's a phenomenon no one ever tells you.

More sunlight or solar power equals more masculine energy for hitting home runs. The light energy will help transmute dark, stagnant, negative energy blockages lingering for whatever reason and blocking the flow. I cannot emphasize enough, the importance of high energy in order to hit home runs often. People must have solar energy to survive and the more one can harness, the better.

The inner monologue is a large factor in shaping your reality. Words are powerful. Pay attention to the words repetitively crossing your mind. Speak positively about yourself. These words mold the experiences in life. Treat your mind with respect and remember you are the master and it is your servant.

The critical negative internal voice feeds off of negativity. Producing positive mental words will gradually silence this voice until the negative monster withers away.

The mind is a breeding ground for any experience you choose to bestow. It is important to act humble and think confidently. I thought to myself, "I am a better hitter." I didn't verbalize it. Plenty of people and scenarios tested this affirmation, but I kept thinking it while my level of play constantly elevated.

Energy is really phonetic code for inner G. The letter G symbolizes the golden ratio spiral. The inner spiral is the inspiring force in each one of us. Home run kings are inspirers with an enormous bandwidth for energy or inner G.

Their abundant energy reserves are readily available at a moments notice. Unfortunately, this wealth of abundant force can be squandered. It happens to many hitters unknowingly. It happens through supplication and the usurping of energy. It is more beneficial to keep our own energy life force for our mission, in this case, hitting ridiculous amounts of home runs.

Avoid all religions. They will limit thinking. These mind controlling dogmatic institutions will slowly indoctrinate people to a mediocre set of beliefs. Home run superstars subscribe to strong empowering beliefs. There is much more attainable than what the average religious person believes to be. All religions have their partial truths and benefits, but a religion will hinder what a hitter thinks is possible.

Catastrophic amounts of people have died in the name of religion. It's no surprise the Holy Wars were fought to feed these parasitic spiritual entities. The word "religion" means to legion again. It means to separate people into legions. Legions fight in wars.

Fear is a feeling of separation. So, more separation equals more fear. To hit home runs consistently, a hitter must feel the polar opposite of fear, which is love and experience oneness or wholeness. The hitter must be a coherent force.

When coherent, there is much less negative mental chatter and self-destructive obstacles in the hitter's way. Love quickens the integration of wholeness.

Any type of religion or cult can connect with an individual's energy and prey on portions of it. There are esoteric contracts with the deity and religious members. This is arcane knowledge usually hidden from the members. Even if you've left your religion and don't practice or attend anymore, your energy can and is still being drained.

Home run hitter's must retain as much of their personal energy and power as possible and not give it to a deity. Beware of the baptism ritual. I was baptized near age 13. It is an initiation ritual into membership. It is magic. Gradually the new member's energy is syphoned off for the deity to use how it pleases. Home runs won't come as often when the person is subjected to regular life force energy harvesting.

Religions are cults. Although there is a negative connotation with cults it is not necessarily good or bad. I don't like endorsing the duality of good and bad. It is however, mostly bad for people blindly engaging in one. The ignorant is usually taken advantage of in cults. I do not condone joining any religion. However, connecting with Christ in my heart and mind has helped throughout my life's journey.

Once a person becomes aware of this shocking truth about religions, the leeching can be stopped. Writing down or reciting an energetic severance is enough to end this exploitation. Contracts and agreements must be clearly understood by both parties or it is a breach. A declaration like the one below or a variation of it can be used successfully.

I ask for all attachments, contracts, cords, entities, hooks, implants, soul ties, thought creations, thought forms, thought patterns no longer serving my higher good be cut, removed and healed going past, present, and future across all aspects of self, dimensions, lives and timelines.

People, sexual encounters, items, entertainment, movies, television shows, music, video games, productions, ideas, companies, coworkers, fraternities, sororities, organizations and all entities attached to them be cut and sealed. I ask for all usurped energy to be returned to me, the rightful owner upon the severance. I ask that this severing and sealing occur in the natural, in the spirit, and in every other realm, known and unknown. It is done.

In addition, ask your higher self for everything deposited in your mind, memory, will, emotions, body, soul and spirit to be thoroughly scrubbed clean. Ask for anything taken from you: spiritual gifts, virtues, things known and unknown be fully restored.

5

The consistent home run hitter possesses a high emotional quotient. Emotional intelligence empowers the hitter for habitual home run hitting. There is a correlation with high EQs and higher income. Baseball is a lucrative profession. High EQ is paramount in making a lucrative career in baseball.

The game is full of rejection. The brain equates rejection to physical pain. Getting out more often than getting hits is painful. Enough rejection adds up to more traumas for the person to carry around and eventually deal with to release. The emotional anguish gets stuck in the body. This makes it easy to get caught up in slumps in baseball. Baseball players have to be emotionally intelligent in order to survive and succeed.

Transmuting emotions is crucial for athletic success. Becoming a master of emotional alchemy creates a powerful home run hitter. Turning base emotions such as fear, anger, or despair into higher emotions is most certainly worthwhile. Imagining the pleasurable result of hitting the home run is potent fuel for manifesting it. First feel the emotions about the current results. Then imagine and feel the emotions about the desired result as if it has happened.

Embodying presence means to go into and feel all of these base emotions and release them. A person who does this routinely will be more coordinated, less tense, and more athletically inclined. The life force will flow throughout the body and home runs will fly out of the park with ease.

When a person loses presence of the moment it is usually from avoiding feeling a painful emotion and causes dissociation. To stay connected to oneself these emotions must be dealt with or a disconnection happens and the stagnant emotional energy essentially blocks the soul from shining through and manifesting dreams in our physical reality.

We all have our shit to handle and deal with sooner or later. It's there waiting for us and won't go away just because we ignore it. Anyone who wants to revel in the glory of hitting home runs like an MVP is courageous and deals with problems, whether emotional or any type of problem as soon as possible.

The Art of Hitting Home Runs

Emotions are energy in motion. Well, until they are trapped and suppressed by us. They require release and movement. Once emotions are freed, so are you. The longer we wait to deal with these problems or traumas, the more carnage we attract into our life. When they get stuck inside, they cause problems because there is no motion. These little stagnant bundles of emotionally charged energy lodged in our bodies wreak havoc in an effort to be acknowledged, accepted and released.

The home run king stays present and experiences these emotions to transmute the energy and let the energetic current circulate better. Not staying present and dwelling on the negative emotions gives the mind and ego an opportunity to dominate the experience. This cannot happen to consistently hit homers. Do not listen to negative self-talk.

It is better to not think at all during the at-bat. Overconfidence is not the home run hitter's friend. It feeds the ego validation and shuts down the divine energetic presence. Hitting home runs requires humble confidence. Knowing there is a pitch to hit out every game with absolute conviction solidifies this humbly confident state of being. This state of being makes the hitter relaxed and still actively seeking to find an excellent pitch, instead of resting on laurels.

Once the excellent pitch is found, rotating the hips ahead of the hands and shoulders stretches the core muscles, which facilitates them to powerfully contract and whip the shoulders around as the bat penetrates the strike zone.

I recommend avoiding as many substances as possible in order to keep the energy and emotional intelligence high in the body.

Alcohol will dismantle the energy. Several days of recovery are required for the hitter to become grounded again. The energy levels are depleted, the body is less present, the aura is less bright and spirit is less embodied than before imbibing.

We all know of people who can go out drinking and function well the next day or even while drinking in athletics, business, various art forms or whatever the case may be. This happens because this person is releasing stuck feelings holding them back from easily achieving their goal. So in humble moderation, it can be helpful. It's not sustainable for putting up copious home run statistics though.

Caffeine is another hindering substance. Routine use of it is widely accepted in our society. People tend to dismiss it. They forget it actually isn't healthy. It is a drug. It constricts the body and energy flow. Muscles contract and twitch when too much is ingested. Tension is higher and the blood flow is constricted. Dilated blood vessels make hitting much easier. A relaxed hitter is normally a better hitter. It's more advantageous to stay mostly calm and relaxed at the plate before the wind-up.

Being in a state of serenity clears a pathway for a current to flow through. Caffeine and other substances make unnecessary tensions. The tension weighing over the back leg is all the hitter wants. Harboring it in the back leg and releasing it breaks the tension with a full on eruption on the baseball. A slight counter rotation occurs while the hitter loads up prior to the explosive contact. If there is any at all, depending on whether or not the nanosecond decision is made to swing.

Marijuana is more complex. A great home run hitter avoids it because he is operating at such a high level and doesn't want the substance to lower him. If the inevitable occurs and the hitter goes through a slump, marijuana can help the hitter become present and raise his vibe. It is useful for establishing equilibrium for a person, meaning it will higher or lower vibrations depending on the state of the person prior to usage.

Players can benefit from a cerebral enhancing marijuana strain because it is complementary to an active lifestyle, opposed to a sedating strain. It doesn't usually help during a season long home run streak. In fact, it will most likely slow down the streak by capping hitting ability. Using it will temporarily expand the aura and accelerate healing. Unfortunately, it can puncture one's aura and cause energy leakage, making the user dependent on it to remain uplifted.

The cannabidiol (CBD) is a natural remedy found in cannabis with a plethora of health benefits. It is not psychoactive. There are neuroprotective properties in CBD and could improve overall well being. It might be wise to use this exclusively.

Back in the 2008 Major League Baseball All-Star home run derby, recovering heroin addict and alcoholic Josh Hamilton set the record for most home runs in a single round by hitting a mind blowing 28 homers. His life force energy was flowing better because he remained sober. And it was easier to slay the home run game.

A healthy sober person has greater abilities to manifest. Most unnatural substances are basically a toxic sludge and will clog the person's system on multiple levels. By no longer ingesting toxic substances Hamilton's energy was not dwindling, making him empowered again. He was a talented baseball player operating at a high performance level before giving up substance abuse, but his radical success was astounding once he rid himself of the toxicity.

All of these substances crowd a hitter's natural energy and become part of the ego, which makes blockages. Removing these from the body makes the hitter open and vulnerable. Output becomes second nature; a default setting. Hitting home runs is the result of a person putting their essence out into reality.

Substance use makes a person numb. The numbness shuts off the emotional guidance system and disconnects the hitter from the true source of power within. It's imperative to have it running to hit well. The internal navigation must be online for pitch selecting, because it is linked to the intuition. It is basically a home run hitting compass.

6

Always be acting offensive in the batter's box. An offensive player is actually a vulnerable one. When batters get 2 strikes, they will occasionally change their approach just to make contact. They get defensive. A home run hitter doesn't do this or his output will diminish. Staying offensive keeps the hitter exposed and vulnerable. Vulnerability is true strength.

Even playing defense in the field is better done from an offensive mind-set. When a ball is hit to defensive players, they act offensive by charging toward the ball. Most hitters close off, tense up and act defensive when hitting isn't going well. This is a constrictive approach for a hitter. It is detrimental and suppresses the channeling of the body's energy and the self. A home run king knows his value is abundant and lets it flow outward. There is always a way to hit a homer.

I like a 32" or 33" bat, but have more home run success with the shorter length. I advise using a lighter bat than a heavier one. It's a common

The Art of Hitting Home Runs

misconception bigger bats hit the ball harder or farther. I have not found this to be true whatsoever. Finding the most comfortable bat size is better, even if it feels too small or light. Bat speed means less than one might think. Timing a pitch is more important.

    Establish the right bat grip. The manner in which you hold the handle of a homerun stick alters the speed and intensity of your hit. I was told by many people to let my hands have a loose grip, but instead held a moderately tight one. I had to retape the bat handle gripping often because of it. Choking up on the handle, holding the bat nearer to the barrel quickens bat swing speed yet loses power. I held near the base of the bat for less speed but to gain powerful momentum.

    One of the greatest home run hitters of all time is Babe Ruth. He was known to practically grind his bat into sawdust at the plate. He was asked about how to hit home runs, and said the ball will go further; the harder he grips the bat.

There are plenty of nasty pitchers out there. Never get intimidated by flaming fastballs or wicked curve balls. Those pitches are spinning with more revolutions, meaning more energy is already in the baseball from the pitcher. Less oomph is required from the batter to hit the ball deep out of the park.

Take ownership at the plate. Babe Ruth did. He owned himself fully. Raised at an orphanage, he wasn't raised with the same sense of being owned like a child raised by biological parents. Orphans don't feel the same protection and containment of a child with two healthy loving parents. However orphans don't experience the negative aspect of having parents and being owned either.

The parents control individuality. Many times the parents identify with the child as extensions of their egos. They want to possess them and have them live a life for them.

Babe Ruth experienced being disowned like an orphan. This gave him freedom to hit home runs for him, not a parent. No one possessed him and lived through him, so he truly loved the game for himself. Hitting home runs for a significant other, parent or anyone else that may own the hitter in any capacity results in less home run productivity. The home run hitter must exude dominance by owning the situation in its entirety. He hits home runs for himself over anyone else. This is his focus.

The Art of Hitting Home Runs

    Living a life for anyone other than oneself is inauthentic and throws a person off of their masculine core. When a hitter wants to do well for anyone else, even for a manager or fans before his own volition, he is losing authenticity and caring what others think. This is not in alignment with a high value masculine essence required to hit home runs incessantly. He is living to be liked. Home run hitters do not care about being liked by anyone. They will not trade their value in exchange for the validation of being liked.

Contrary to popular opinion, routinely hitting home runs is not usually a competitive act. It's a high vibrational lifestyle. All emotions emit a frequency. Competitiveness is almost neutral. It can be negative on the spectrum of emotions because it creates duality and comparison. Thus, a winner and loser and a hierarchy is formed. It's a linear and archaic resonance and limits the player's home runs.

    The competitiveness frequency will raise a person out of depression, so people may think it is good. It is not favorable for a home run king though. Thinking about another player's performance or even your own in game is toxic for home run totals. The more present the hitter is, the less he'll be concerned with his actual totals anyway. His confidence will reach such an elevated level that every single at-bat becomes a realistic opportunity to hit a home run. Though this may be fleeting. It is an ecstatic state of being.

When a mechanical tweak must happen for a player, make adjustments before the game. Then let it go. Move focus to another area of hitting to improve and repeat the pattern. What happens here is the brain and body makes adjustments when the mind isn't intensely focused on it. Never think about any of this at the plate. Make the adjustments, and the brain can adapt overnight. It's similar to studying for an exam and retaining more of the information the next day after sleeping.

Musicians do the same thing. I've noticed this when practicing guitar. I'll learn a new song, sleep on it, and play better the following day after resting. The adjustment just needs time to integrate. Keeping the body detoxified and integrated eases this process. Baseball is similar to playing an instrument, except hitters are using a bat as an instrument, of course. On a grand scale the better we play our human instrument the easier life becomes to navigate.

This may be common sense to take excellent care of the physical body, but many baseball players neglect their physical health and fitness. When a hitter takes better care of his body and his environment, he'll hit more home runs. People may argue about having success and not caring about health or fitness, but those people don't grasp how powerful they really are. Their potential is so much greater.

Exercise will keep the brain healthy and sharp. I've discovered exercising several times a week for the cognitive benefits over the physical benefits makes it easier to find sustaining motivation. The home run hitter will do well with most any type of exercise as long as there is additional blood flow and neurotransmitters in the brain. It doesn't necessarily need to be a hitting exercise.

During physical strength training I recommend listening to music. Anything fast-paced and motivating is amazing for working out. It activates the adrenaline. Aggressive music with excessive bass spurs muscle growth. Listening to music in the dugout before heading to the on-deck circle drowns out the distractions and amps focus.

I've found music tuned to a certain frequency can entrain the body back to an optimal tuning. Songs tuned in 432 Hz instead of traditional concert tuning of 440 Hz restores the body's natural resonance with the universe. Most modern songs are

440 Hz. The alteration in Hz was intended to make songs more exciting, but puts the body out of sync. Listening to any music tuned to 432 Hz will give the hitter's system a reset back to a cool, calm and confident demeanor. The biorhythm will be ideal and cycling the bases regularly will eventually become the new normal.

The increasingly more popular float tanks are beneficial for physical and emotional health. Spending time in the tank is excellent for visualization. It's like meditation on steroids. Professional athletes on championship caliber teams are floating weekly or even more often. The Chicago Cubs, New England Patriots, and Golden State Warriors all embrace floating.

Spending an hour in a float tank will keep the hitter's mind open. Emotional health will improve greatly and the physical body will be at ease. I've noticed the physiological effect of increased saliva production while floating. It's indicative of the parasympathetic nervous system activating. The PNS is the body's healing system. Past traumas may come up to be released. It could be letting go of the shame of a recent game where the hitter is 0-5 with three strikeouts.

The Art of Hitting Home Runs

    Staying open makes the hitter present, so tension must be released to maintain this state. Tension means the body is holding on to something from the past or bracing itself for the future. Neither the past nor the future are taking place right now and aren't in the present moment. Tensions eventually melt away when the hitter remains present. The process of thoroughly shinning the soul through the physical vessel happens in the moment. This lets the energy flow through the body for hitting home runs as intended. All home runs happen in the now.

7

Any additional attention brought to a situation feeds it. Attention is energy and provides a boost. Crowds and media can amplify the electricity of a field or stadium. At age 12, my mother video recorded all of my games. It improved my performance because I was receiving additional energy from the camera.

One who is aware and receptive to other people's energies can use it to his advantage to manifest the reality of his choosing. A fan cheering with a simple open hand gesture and an intense flare for his team's success will create intent and an outpouring of raw energy emanates from the fan's hands and aura.

Tournaments always bring more onlookers to see the games. I performed at a higher level during tournaments because there are more fans in attendance. More spectators are generally better for the home team. It always makes a subtle difference in the players because the fans are giving their energy and intention toward the team they're rooting for, usually the home team.

The Art of Hitting Home Runs

Everyone can benefit from support and encouragement and athletes are no different. This makes the players a type of medium for the fans to live through.

Often times having another star player on the team is mutually beneficial for both players. People may dismiss it as a friendly competition, but it's more about the aforementioned entrainment of high frequency play. To reiterate, a gold ring or high frequency stone will likely stay at that wavelength and a person will entrain up to it.

Two star players basking in one another's orbit for a long enough time will begin to display a similar resonance and even produce similar offensive statistics. This is enormously beneficial for hitting home runs. If you want to become a great home run king, start playing alongside one.

Professional star athlete's who get more media coverage greatly benefit from the attention, amping up performance. Attention gives the person validation to continue being a unique individual. It provides the athlete with more internal security. The more love a person gets from others, the better off that person's life will be. Even loving a person and not telling them will positively influence their life.

Star players are obviously exposed to more influx of energies than an average person. Some of these energies are malevolent, but mostly the players receive a nurturing energetic environment full of love and attention. The professional sports leagues understand the importance of media, both the dark and light aspects of it.

Popular home run hitters and numerous professional athletes are known to get shoe endorsement deals with a brand. In some cases the athlete may get a standalone personal brand. Aside from the obvious monetary benefit from a brand endorsement, is the subtle energetic boost from the logo.

When a player has a personal logo, it draws additional energy and attention to the athlete. Any time a person acknowledges it, even unaware of whose logo it is, the athlete receives energy. The athlete is literally growing more powerful from the logo. Corporations utilize this tactic to reap extraordinary benefits.

Home run hitter's who actually get branded with a juggernaut company are extremely rare.

The Art of Hitting Home Runs

Every hitter can utilize this concept free of the contract. Creating a symbol with the right intent can help influence reality.

A player can design a simple logo by writing a small phrase, like "I am a powerful home run king". Then the intention is set within the sentence. Remove all the vowels from the words. Keep breaking down the sentence until there are only a few letters remaining. Use those lines of the letters to construct the personal symbol. It doesn't matter what letters are used to mold into the design. The most important ingredient is the intention and it is set instantly.

Once the logo is created, the player doesn't even have to remember the exact words used to help create it. The next step is keeping it in vision daily or weekly at the very least. Putting it in a wallet is a great idea. Drawing the logo on batting gloves is brilliant. The intention is embedded in the conception of the design for anyone who views it. This is an ancient tactic for manifestation. Make sure to keep it visible. Over time and seeing it repetitively, the mental intention will make an imprint on life and reality.

People don't even have to believe in the power of symbols for one to work. The manifestation from the logo's intention will take place regardless. Getting a logo made for an athlete will have a positive psychological effect, even for a skeptic.

Attention is a form of energy. Since the logo represents the player, any time attention is paid to it, the player is gaining energy. It gives a renewed confidence no matter how well the hitter is already performing. Wearing a known athletic brand associated with a successful home run hitter or just a player you admire can have this same psychological effect too. The personal logo is more powerful though.

We've all heard thousands of times throughout our lives about the importance of eating healthy fruits and vegetables to live well. It is true. To take your power hitting to the next level, eat more fruits and vegetables.

Eat a vegan regimented meal plan. Not only does it dramatically help our planet's environment (one person eating a plant-based diet saves about 1100 gallons of water per day), but it enhances athletic ability and coordination too. It may sound counterintuitive, but many vegan athletes are actually physically stronger. I can attest firsthand to increased strength just from giving up meat alone and eating vegetarian foods.

Many professional athletes credit superior performance to the raw plant-based vegan diet. NBA champion Kyrie Irving eats a plant-based diet along with many others, including bodybuilders. Vegan fighter, Nate Diaz, defeated former UFC Featherweight Champion Conor McGregor (undefeated at the time) with overwhelming ferocity, pace and energy.

Consuming healthy foods clear up the body's system. This includes clearing the mind. Fruits and veggies provide mental clarity and aid the intuition in reading situations more accurately. As the awareness increases, picking up on people's intentions becomes easier. Life becomes lucid. This comes in handy when reading a pitcher. Eating a plant-based diet is simple, not necessarily easy, just like the art of hitting home runs.

Mastering the long ball is a result of efficient energy use more than physical strength. Eating dense, low vibrational foods, like meat inhibits energy flow and distorts the intuition. Anything a person consumes can make an impression, especially foods. Dense foods are cancerous and lead to dense thoughts. Hitting home runs often doesn't happen from repetitive exposure to a dense cancerous environment. It occurs when the hitter comes from a virile, thriving state of being and makes an impression on the environment.

The physical body is a system. All foods make a small impact on it. When the physical system is operating efficiently, the hitter performs with ease. A hitter must be fluid and highly capable of adapting in a nanosecond. Nothing is more fluid than water. Fruits and veggies are mostly water just like a human being. So regular intake keeps the hitter fluid. A fluid hitter moves well and doesn't get stuck in slumps for long. His body adapts like an organic, well-oiled machine with silky smooth mechanical transitions.

Monitoring food consumption will net exceptional progress for the aspiring home run king. All food has information for the body to read, download and use. Everything consumed changes the body's system to a degree. Notice all personal consumption, including music and television. Improving upon it is a step in individual evolution for creating a thriving lifestyle where hitting home runs is almost as easy as exhaling.

People are programmed to believe protein is more important in muscle strength than it really it is. The human body gets plenty of protein from fruits and vegetables alone. Eating fruits and vegetables until I feel satisfied noticeably enhances my coordination. The recommended daily value is fabricated by big businesses to increase profits. The importance of protein is minimal in building adequate muscle strength for optimal athletic performance.

Fruits and veggies absorb more solar energy; more light. Solar energy equals masculine energy for power hitting.

8

In the past I neglected the idea of feng shui and unknowingly suffered from it. The external reality is a reflection of the internal one. When I was 12, I was unaware of feng shui, but I was actively practicing it. I loved cleaning. Vacuuming was a pleasurable habit for me. I made sure my room was free of clutter and organized. I stayed super clean as a 12 year old. It paid dividends well beyond my expectations in baseball.

Feng shui is related to hitting home runs because it frees up the energy flow in a space both within and without. Less clutter clears space for expansion in other areas of our lives, not only the physical. Each time you remove a mess, dirt, debris, or anything you don't really like about a physical space, it clears mental blockages inside simultaneously.

Cleanliness is divine. Making the living space clean eases the subconscious. Vacuum weekly, and invest in an air purifier and shower filter to reduce fluoride for optimal health.

The Art of Hitting Home Runs

I felt so happy from cleaning I would even go vacuum my sister's room. It was absolutely liberating. I've experienced the overwhelming stuck feeling of a messy environment. The hardest part is actually putting the cleaning in motion by making the decision to get up and declutter. It's always relieving. Once you gain momentum, the dopamine rush sparks you and extra tasks tend to get accomplished.

Consider becoming a minimalist. The stuff we have gets tied into the ego. Most people think this stuff is who they are, but that's false. It's an attachment. Sentimental things are not easy to get rid of, but those things take us out of the present and into the past. Home runs are hit in the now. I advise staying away from too many sentimental objects.

Less stuff easily enables the true essence of who we really are to radiate outward. Minimizing stuff keeps life simple. Simplicity is brilliance. It allows the genius within to come forth. I believed this wholeheartedly in my approach to hitting home runs. Getting bogged down by all the details of mechanics, the interworking of the situation or overanalyzing a baseball swing complicates the process. Simplicity is a secret to success. It's really simple to hit home runs. The framework of the entire strategy is charging the energy and swinging intuitively.

There isn't a batting stance I believe is perfect for everyone. If it feels more comfortable then do it. As long as the energy is charged in the rear calf, the hitter can personalize the rest of the stance and swing. I prefer to be deeper in the batter's box. I keep my feet even and like to crowd the plate by standing only a couple inches from the chalk line.

There isn't a favorable pitch location for hitting a home run. Obviously when a pitcher throws one right down the middle of the strike zone, it is sinful for him. When it's in the strike zone, it can be hit over the outfield wall. Many hitters love pulling the ball. I like hitting to all parts of the field. Going with the pitch is better. I occasionally use an inside out swing. I don't mind hitting it to the opposite field.

Going with the pitch is natural when in the flow state of being. Since I don't have a preference for the pitch or area of the field, it keeps me open to slugging out from any pitch location. I don't mind breaking ball pitches or fastballs either. Adapting to pitches is a key to becoming a consistent power hitter. All pitches can be turned into home runs.

Great power hitters do not swing level to the ground. They tilt.

The head of the bat drops down below the hands during the swing. This allows pitches down in the strike zone to be dealt with accordingly while the hips are powerfully rotated.

It's typical for a home run hitter to have an uppercut swing and I certainly do. An uppercut will organically make a long fly ball trajectory happen. Digging in with the rear foot in the batter's box instantly makes the swing more of an uppercut because the batter is not exactly level on the ground anymore. It improves the launch angle. It will be easier to put plenty of backspin on the ball, making it soar higher in the air. Backspin makes moon shots fly off your bat.

It makes no sense to swing level because the strike zone is not level. It is lower than the hitter. Digging in and having a slight uppercut will put the bat in alignment with the pitch for a longer period of time. It might be only a fraction of a second longer, but certainly makes a significant difference in the likelihood of striking the ball with an explosive impact in the sweet spot of the bat. Making contact is easier too because the pitcher throws at a downward angle instead of level, so a level swing is less probable for hitting the ball out of the park.

Numerous people discuss full extension as though it is revolutionary to a renowned swing. In all actuality, extension is the result of an optimal swing opposed to the cause of one. In a sweet swing, the front elbow and shoulder is closed and the movements remain minimal, boosting the rate at which the shoulders turn. The hands are rotating in relative association with, the back shoulder.

Baseball is a game with two opposing teams. Within the teams are many different players or aspects of the team. For an individual player embarking on the path of a sensational home run hitter, his mind must not have opposing forces to achieve the desired success. The player may have all the mechanics and technical aspects of playing mastered, but this is a small part of success.

Everyone in the field at the professional level appears to have the required skill set to produce successful results. However the mind must be free of conflicting thoughts, beliefs and actions not serving the goal. It must get rid of resistance and become integrated. Talent, luck, fate, or even hard work are small factors in manifesting a goal compared to a person who is living free of resistance to it.

The Art of Hitting Home Runs

There could be self-sabotaging resistance in the mind causing a player to fail. This occurs predominantly on a subconscious level, but in the conscious mind as well. Resisting is a tricky cognitive dissonance. Both aspects of the resistance are forms believing they are favoring the best interests of the sole person. Breaking down the word resistance means to re-insist or asking for you to come after it again.

Giving attention to the resistance feeds it energy and grows it. It is normal in baseball or any competition to have a resistance for the sake of the game. However internally, the player must not have to try to dominant the inner conflict because it only feeds it.

A team can overpower another team, but a player can't overpower oneself internally. If there is an aspect of oneself who doesn't actually want to succeed then success can be neutralized. There are 9 players on the baseball field. It's comical to imagine, but if some of those aspects of the team or players don't want to win and sabotage the team, there is a large possibility of failure. This resistance to success and winning occurs within athletes quite often.

It is vital to be free of all resistance. There isn't focus when a person has conflicting beliefs. Hitting well requires as much focus as possible. The subconscious will focus on the resistance and feed it. Every fiber of the hitter's being must love and truly be committed to hitting home runs.

If the entire being is fragmented, utilizing a coach or counselor is beneficial. Sorting this out alone can help too. Talk about or write down the conscious beliefs not serving the goal. Often times a mental truce can take place just from acknowledging perspectives with friction. Literally have a dialogue with these beliefs to gain a clear understanding of the psychological pulls happening.

Awareness is beautiful. As more resistance is made conscious, one might find a cascade of synchronicities or even miracles ensue. The impossible becomes almost effortless. Once fully integrated, the hitter can hit home runs each game. And, the farthest home runs can surprisingly be the ones with the least amount of effort expelled.

The Art of Hitting Home Runs

9

Whether it's hitting home runs or finding success in any forum, there could be a mental block within stopping you from having the success you truly dream of achieving. People are afraid of success. They know failure. It is like failure is their friend keeping people comfortable and barricading success. Not only do these mental blocks need removed for cranking baseballs yonder or whatever it may be, but being really successful at crushing home runs means, handling pleasure.

This sounds humorous at first. However handling pleasure is not necessarily easy. New circles of people and experiences are drawn to a fierce home run hitter and not all people have the faculties ready to deal with it.

Sports bring people together who might not have otherwise gathered. They distract, dumb-down, yet inspire. An athlete who performs at an extremely high level gives the audience the camaraderie of marveling at the display of one physically and psychologically playing the game well.

Hitting a home run is enjoyably simple. People who don't find that so yet, must dig deeper into their lifestyle and refine it. This is like tuning up the mechanics of the swing. Small deep-rooted alterations can have monumental impact.

A star home run hitter is noble. He is aware of his influence. He is in alignment with the abiding energy sourced within. Bringing together all the aspects of oneself creates a fusion for optimal athletic performance. Furthermore the crowd reinforces this fusion and reciprocates with synergy between the onlookers, team and star player. The collective spirit is embodied actively for those of us involved in any type of sport, whether it's playing or spectating.

What a great home run hitter can do for the game is profound. Most people do not realize the philosophical undertones in baseball. It is just a concrete and physical game to the unaware. When a home run king emerges or even a simple magnificent play happens, it is a sign of integration of the spirit and the physical. Star players know how to ground themselves and embrace both materiality and spirituality. Denying either is unwise. When a player transcends the average status quo and showcases greatness, it is quintessentially divine.

The Art of Hitting Home Runs

Hitting home runs really is an art. It's remarkable to see a player who has command of his body in a consistently advantageous manner. If one aspires to be a legend in the game of baseball, one must be disciplined and operate in a moral framework. He or she is aware of the capability for self-sabotaging savagery, yet chooses to perform well for a higher cause. Playing at an elite level raises everyone's vibration regardless of the player's reasoning for playing great. Thus, uplifting the team, fans and society at large.

There is a sophisticated level of collaboration with other humans happening when a player hits home runs. It's an admirable quality to play well with other people and still manifest the desired result. This is adaptable and dominant simultaneously. The act of hitting a home run is spontaneous. The pitcher can throw anything at him and the ball could easily end up as a souvenir in the seats for a four-bagger. This is a powerful skill of surgeon-like precision. We all can acquire it.

I've personally experienced fluctuations in my ability to apply precise spontaneity based on my current embodiment of spirit. Wielding this skill consistently is attained through mastery of the self.

I've harped several times on the vital component of a true home run hitter, loving it. Loving the act of homering removes the attachment of expectation. It makes it more enjoyable because expectation is inverted to happiness. Don't expect to hit one, or the love of actually hitting it will dissipate.

Any amount of home runs is enough. This belief makes the hitter feel adequate and prone to blasting steadfast long balls. When a person really loves hitting homers, it will happen. The internal love of it can put the next most dangerous hitter in the game into the process of gestation.

Self-love and loving your actions is miracle making. Thinking about fortune, fame, validation, proving self-worth, making a parent proud or significant other happy takes a person out of the heart space and up in the mind; fracturing the focus.

Hit home runs for yourself over everyone else. It places the proverbial home run crown on your head. Playing the game imbued with love is beautiful. Before you realize it, you might be a living legend or inspire the player who becomes one.

Made in the USA
Columbia, SC
24 November 2018